T0064563

LESSONS

FROM LEARNING TO LIVING

TONI OSBORNE

authorHOUSE®

AuthorHouse™
1663 Liberty Drive
Bloomington, IN 47403
www.authorhouse.com
Phone: 1 (800) 839-8640

Published by AuthorHouse   07/21/2015

ISBN: 978-1-5049-2297-5 (sc)
ISBN: 978-1-5049-2296-8 (e)

Print information available on the last page.

This book is printed on acid-free paper.

CONTENTS

ABOUT THE AUTHOR

What if I told you something that could change the course of your life; forever? What if I helped to equip you with the tools you need to more efficiently navigate your way through the obstacles and pitfalls in life?

I am someone that has learned many lessons the hard way, and due to that, I'm determined to spare everyone the same hardships. My name is Toni Osborne, and I am a mother, telecommunications professional, police officer, author—and no stranger to extenuating circumstances.

In this book you will find my original quotes and the expansion of my thoughts as they relate to the quotes. The quotes are a culmination of the life-changing revelations that have come out of my very own experiences; each truism having enormous potential to not only enrapture you, but ultimately propel you to an awakening in areas of your life where that may be needed.

In all my roles I am the rock and the voice of reason. I have witnessed my advice, leadership, and example, help to change lives. If you're willing, I'm sure I can guide you over a few hurdles of your own.

This book is dedicated to its inspiration: my children—Justin, Taylor, Sydney, and Anthony. The only reason I ever strived to do my best is because they were watching.

ACKNOWLEDGMENTS

Thank you heavenly Father, thank you Jesus, and thank you Holy Spirit…for everything.

Thank you, family—Grandmother QC Rosebud and Great-Aunt Johnnie Marie—for your prayers and constant covering. I thank my children, my mother, Miriam; sisters, LaTrina and Stacey; brothers-in-law, Stacy and Chris, and cousin Kazz, for letting me share my dreams with you. Your listening ears and watchful eyes keep me on my grind, and knowing that you guys always have my back is the wind beneath my wings. (It also doesn't hurt that you keep my secrets!) I thank my nieces, Christina, Ryan, and Jordan; nephews Mario, Jaleel, and Jaylin; and all the rest of you Osborne/Finley's near and far, here and gone, for your love and encouragement. You have no idea how much you motivate me.

Thank you, extended family—Henry Earl and Beverly Joyce—for your example and commitment to family, Aunt Jackie for your wise counsel, Grandma Sis for your prayers, steadfastness, and that amazing coconut pound cake, yes! And all the rest of the White family for your open arms and awesome love for me and the children, it has meant everything to me. And to you Terry, my friend and partner in parenting; what a remarkable team we are! The children have tried and tried to penetrate our united front but to no avail. We ain't no punks! Lol.

Thank you, God family—Niccole and Aaron, Janice and Curtis, Grandma, Grandpa Fred, and our mom, Penny; how full my experience has been because you are in it. The love Mom gave us was incomparable, and grandma's Friday night fried catfish and spaghetti was a force to be reckoned with! These thoughts keep me sane.

Thank you, Maxwell family— sisters Carmelita, Danielle, Tammie, and Ericka, all of my wonderful nieces and nephews, and in memory of my late brother Brandon. I know we had a late start, but I'd rather have had that than a missed opportunity. The abundance of family is truly a blessing, and I look forward to us growing, building, learning, and loving from here on out.

Thank you, friends—Johnetta and Shona. It's been a whole lotta years, ladies! Who knew our childhood friendship would blossom into the grown-woman fabulousness it is today? Thank you for all the things I couldn't put in this book (smile). I plan to ride this thing right on out; with you. Jolanda, the first half of the "Power Puff girls" (lmbo!) You are the eyes in the back of my head and truly one of *thee* most sincere people I know. Well, except when you're selling me out for Danny's key lime pie, but we don't have to talk about that if you don't want to. I'm honored to have your friendship☺. Falana, you don't know it, but for years, God has used you as a spiritual guide for me through our friendship. I sooo appreciate your transparency, unwavering support, love, prayers, and the mighty woman of God that you are! Thanks for inviting me to visit your church on that fateful day; my life has never been the same.

Thank you, Robyn Williams. The way we met was truly orchestrated by Him. (Divine connections are real, people!) The details of that meeting always bring a smile to my face, as they serve to remind me of God's ever-presence and real-time activity in our lives. Oh and, about that challenge you posed, well… turns out it was exactly what I needed!

Thank you, Alain Locke family. I'll be forever grateful to you—Pat Ryan, Lennie Jones, Gloria Woodson, Patrick Love, Vonyell Foster, Mia Stokes, and the host of phenomenal educators and assisting staff members at our school. When the children and I first walked through those doors I could not have imagined the rich relationship we'd build. The stellar education and organizational success that has developed over the last fourteen years has been nothing short of amazing. Thank you for taking us along for the ride.

And, without further ado,
Thank you, "Life" — for material.

My Prayer for You

Thank you, Father, for this powerful release, that through it I might grow, heal, and be strengthened. Please guide my hand as it unfolds the truth in my heart and the depths of my soul.

And Father, if by chance my words fall upon the eyes of others, I pray they find themselves motivated, encouraged, counseled, and consoled; as my writings are a reflection of the talent you've given me, and the gift you're giving them.

In the name of Jesus, my Lord and Savior, I pray.

Thank you, Father, Amen.

My Challenge to You

Advice is good upon implementation.

I have given you a book of truisms—all original in thought and practical in nature. They're simple yet profound, provocative, and penetrating. The quotes beg you to ponder, and precede blank pages on which to pen your thoughts; as questions invite you to delve inside yourself for the answers, for therein they lie.

Be that as it may, "you can lead a horse to water but you can't make him drink" John Heywood has said long-since, and so it goes with you. If you don't put words into action what good is having said them? If you don't put words into action, what good is having heard them?

<u>Do not believe the hype!</u>

You don't have to personally experience every circumstance to learn from it. *Many things can be learned from the experiences of others.* In the end, you cannot deny what you know.

Learn, so you can live!

INTRODUCTION

The Car Ride

It's 4:00 a.m. I'm being coerced out of my slumber by the faint sounds of music I can't stand to listen to. I set the alarm to one particular station with hopes that my annoyance with the music it plays will catapult me out of bed to turn it off and thus, start my day. Once again, that reasoning has proven to be merely theoretical because by 4:30, the alarm clock has transformed into a siren, and when I clumsily reach to shut it off, I knock it over. Now it's blaring, and obnoxiously forces me out of that warm, comfy bed to silence it. Rats!

Now that I'm up, I might as well get this party started. Workout? Done. Kids? Wrangled. Breakfast? Eaten. Supplements? Taken. Bags? Packed. Lunches? Made. Lights? Off. Car fuel? On E as usual; make stop. Time? About 6:30. Okay, it's past 6:30 and we're pressed for time again; alternate routes being calculated in my head as we rush out the door, but no matter. **I'm determined to make this a great day.**

Toni Osborne

Four stops will be made, the first of which is over an hour away via a trek through Chicago's downtown, and that time increases upon the return trip, amid rush hour traffic. This is our life; a regular school/workweek routine, and fourteen years in the making. As taxing as the very thought of this is, this confinement of space and time has surfaced as the most consistent opportunity for me to connect with, and to teach my children. So, for all of you with a five minute commute—my apologies.

We spend so much time in the car between all our obligations that it's become our first home—with a trunk that serves as a kitchen, and a dining room that confuses itself with a backseat; go figure. It is by no means conventional and certainly not for everyone, but the forum is open, and the atmosphere is no holds barred. I have come to know my children; their thoughts, visions, personalities, temperaments, frustrations, hurts, and they have learned mine. During this time I have learned how very blessed we were to have it. It was during this time, that I came to realize there was never enough time to tell them all the things I needed them to know.

I would watch their faces go blank and eyes glaze over from information overload. Eventually, they began to cry out, "Mommy enough!" forcing me to accept that my authoritarian reign would soon be over, while also knowing that at that time, they'd need me as much as ever. I knew I wouldn't always be around, but I wanted to be there for them, always.

You bear the result of my solution in your hands, as my attempt to be there for them is now my attempt to be there for you—always.

This book is *reinforcement* for everyone who wants the blessing of wisdom to resonate in the lives of those they care about. This book is *reaffirmation* for those who have been mentored by everyone, or even only one. This book is *revelation* for those who up until now hadn't had anyone pour into their spirit and fill them with the truth. This book is for all those in *rebellion*; having heard one too many lectures and have a finger in each ear right now … it'll be on the shelf. This book is for you, as I speak to you for every person who has said or would say the same things to you. Receive it, knowing that no matter how far or how long you may stray from what has been imparted to you, it's still in you. You cannot deny what you know.

Learn, so you can live.

INTRODUCTION

The Fundamentals

There are nine keys to living your most fulfilled, well-balanced, and ultimately happy life. If we were cats we'd have one lifetime per key (or so the saying goes), but since we're not, let's take *this* lifetime and successfully combine all nine within it. Come! Time is of the essence.

1. Spiritual (The spirit)
   That place within you that longs to be connected. That void you have that yearns to be filled by something of profound significance. It's that unrelenting desire to be whole and unfragmented; that feeling of emptiness you cannot escape. That is *your* spirit seeking God's spirit.

2. Social (Humanitarianism)
   You inhabit this world and all that is in it with everyone. Take up your cause and let your sense of duty to it be innate, and your allegiance to the betterment of those within the scope of your reach,

impenetrable. You are here on purpose. Let your life make the difference in someone else's.

3. <u>Mental (Psyche/Mindset)</u>
   Few things will help to shape your life more than your perspective. The way we think determines how we feel, and how we feel determines how we function. We're on assignment to battle to the finish with negative thinking patterns; choosing to be positive and optimistic without regard for the circumstances, and in spite of the unknown.

4. <u>Emotional (Heart)</u>
   This is where you can access your innermost being. As a result, you are enlisted to find the balance between being in touch with feeling without being overly sensitive to feeling, and challenged to establish the stability of a steady heartbeat even, and yet especially, among the irregular flow of life.

5. <u>Physical (Body/Temple)</u>
   Your body is your dwelling, at least for now. You must take care to maintain what God has given you, knowing that if it goes undone, you will compromise and substantially limit your functionality and in essence, your impact. *NERSH*: Nourish. Exercise. Rest. Supplement. Hydrate. **NERSH!**

6. <u>Financial (Building Wealth)</u>
   Position yourself to have and not need rather than to need and not have by pursuing financial independence. Start with whatever you have and

build diligently upon that. Do this all of your life. Adopt in your heart the principle of building wealth to be of service and to come to the aid of others; having a clear understanding that the blessing of wealth is not solely for satisfying your every desire, but to assist you in meeting the needs of others.

7. <u>Intellectual(Knowledge/Wisdom)</u>

Controversially, age has not patented wisdom, and youth relinquishes not the expectation of knowledge. Be assured by the sum of your experiences, but place your confidence in the Divinity through which those experiences were afforded. The truest indicator of one's capacity for learning is their acceptance of the lifelong process.

8. <u>Relational (Relationships)</u>

Nothing will have more of an impact on your emotions and state of being, than your relationships. How you relate to others with whom you share this world, more specifically your world, is the key to establishing and maintaining your sanity and inner peace.

9. <u>Passions (Gratification)</u>

If you should learn of all the things that bring a sparkle to your eye,

That soothe your soul and brings a glow upon your face,

If you could know a song that sings of joy unlimited by sky,

Would you then sing to spread that joy in every
place?

If you could see the smiling face receiving gifts from
God through you
Is moved to tears because its heart is set aflame,
Would you lose count of all you'd do henceforth,
ingratiating masses?
Touching souls though you may never know a name.

If you could give them happiness that never loses
its surprise
As they delight and take refuge in what you do,
You'd then embrace your destiny, as to give out, is
to give in,
To what's been placed inside and hides from even
you.

Discover, and release your passions; change the(ir)
world.

CHAPTER 1

Spiritual

Seek God. Find Him.

Our spirit longs to connect with *the* Spirit. For your soul to be at peace, it must find its center there.

- Connect to the Spirit with your heart, mind, and soul.
- Pray for His presence in your life.
- Pray for divine intervention in all things.
- Pray for divine enlightenment and clarity of purpose.
- Believe that He will hear and He will answer.
- Trust that in Him, all things will work for your good.

Falling into alignment with God's plan for others doesn't circumvent your blessings, it enables them.

Make some time and read the poem "Our Deepest Fear" by Marianne Williamson. It brings home this point:

What's for you is for you, and no one but you can stand in the way of that. What other people have is for them; that's why they have it.

None of us owes any apologies for this. God gave you your talents with a specific purpose in mind. You must use your abilities and the resources they generate to elongate your reach and in so doing, you'll not only assist others with their heart's desire, but may coincidentally discover your own.

With that said, render yourself a vehicle for usage in helping to materialize the advancement of others. Be not envious or intimidated by anyone's talents or comeuppance, but to the contrary, be elated; as you are now positioned to be swept up by their blessings due to proximity.

A gift is not for the one granted the ability to give it.

It was not given to me that from it I might receive glory. It was given to me that from it you might receive blessing.

Your talents are not for you, but are to be used *by* you, so that others might be blessed *through* you. They are to be shared with as many people as possible, as you are merely the vessel used by God to pour out this blessing onto others, in the same way that He uses others to pour out blessings onto you. When you accept that great privilege accompanies even greater responsibility, you will more easily step into the role God has destined for you.

Likewise, as others are inspired by your talents, they will become motivated to discover their talents, which will in turn bless others, and so on, and so on, and so on.

My talents are God's gifts to you. Your talents are God's gifts to me.

What are your talents?
And who, specifically, will be gifted by them?

Place your confidence in the Divinity
through which it was afforded.

We are all blessed by God to carry out His purposes for our lives, for each of us has one. We are equipped to produce and called to perform. Be assured that you can do all things through Christ and be certain of your capabilities in Him.

Recognize the power of God in every good deed you do, in every ability you have, and in every*thing* in which you find yourself secure. Regardless of your circumstances, let your greatest hope lie in what God has promised you through what Jesus has done for you.

God is your source.

Jesus is the way. (John 14:6).

Out of the trial comes your magnificence.

If you've ever experienced a hardship, I'm sure at its onset you were convinced it would be the death of you; it would ruin you for sure, right? I know how you feel, but that's all it is—a feeling, not the truth.

The truth is with God on our side we can overcome all things and be better for having gone through them. The truth is; God causes everything to work for our good, even trials.

Allow your ordeals to humble you and by their intrusion, help to create the person in you it is meant for you to become. As you are broken down and rebuilt, acknowledge that it's a great challenge but in your heart, know you will come out on the better side; whatever side.

Transformation is what we undergo when we triumph over our difficult times. Resulting from those victories are newly developed characteristics which serve to equip us for what will be our next level and quite possibly, our next trial.

Accept it as a refining process of sorts, as you make peace with shedding parts of your former self in expectation of your better self. Likewise, be reassured by your growth and the victory in overcoming; for you will be called upon to be a guiding light for someone with a dilemma similar to yours, but their very own.

In the moments with which you are blessed, be present.

I'm all for looking forward and being filled with hope about the days to come. I believe in making plans, and I recognize there is great success in doing so. I've experienced the expectation of a joy-laden future, and used the passing days as fillers until it was realized. I know what it's like to long for night and then long for day and over again, until "that" day has come. I've learned to not wish the day away in anticipation of another; instead to savor it and all it brings, knowing there will be no tomorrow if I miss today.

Spiritual Journal

Toni Osborne

Spiritual Journal

CHAPTER 2

Social

Action is not just for heroes.

"Somebody really needs to change things!"
"I can't wait until they get this taken care of!"
"I'm sure that someone is handling the situation."
"No one's doing *anything* about this!"

Sound familiar? If you haven't said these words I'm sure you've heard them. Truth be told, we'd all rather wait for a hero to show up but the problem is we'd all be waiting for a hero to show up; meanwhile, back at the ranch ...

Needless to say, if you are socially inactive it's definitely not for lack of cause. There's an issue with your name on it *I promise you*, and if you've encountered any adversity firsthand, that area in particular would be a valiant start.

You see, you taking action could make all the difference, because what you have to give may be exactly what is needed. Besides, offering yourself to be of service is in itself heroic. I know that it may seem overwhelming, but you must know that any little thing you do in the way of taking action, propels resolution.

The takeaway is this:

When you open your heart your actions will follow, along with that, your heroism. That someone you're waiting for to do something, is you.

What could use your heroism?

Be inspired by others' desire to emulate you.

This means your light is shining. Someone sees it and is moving toward it. They're drawn to the glow and the warmth of its rays but more than just to witness, they'd like to experience a light with shine so bright; a light of their very own.

Be not annoyed by their attempts to imitate you, instead be flattered by the compliment and be encouraged to further create; as you have now been made aware of your impact on another and the feelings of inspiration it has generated in them.

And incidentally, even when you set the standard, there's nothing like a copycat to spark healthy competition, and make you step up your game.

Who's imitating you?

Responsibility constitutes freedom.

The United States is a country where freedom has been established as a right for everyone, and thankfully so. It's very hard for me to imagine living under the conditions that exist in many other places in the world; as they observe freedom for the elite, taut it as a privilege for the exceptional, and cause it to escape the common.

Notwithstanding these truths freedom is never free, and it unbridled, will cost you everything. Moreover, as you exercise your right to live your life on your terms, be mindful that you share that right with your fellowman, and be respectful of its impending boundaries. It's within our understanding of this fact that freedom reigns, and within our acceptance of this fact that freedom abounds; recognizing that *ignorance does not excuse accountability.*

At the end of the day, no one is at liberty to transgress without its eventual consequence, as freedom is hinged upon that very foundation. At the end of the day, your freedom stops at its potential to violate mine.

Contribute your abilities in support of a cause outside yourself.

Does your existence have impact?
What difference are you going to make in the world?

These are some of the questions you should be asking yourself:

- Have I availed myself of service?
- How will I participate in life?
- Who will I help?
- What will be my cause?
- What will I do to advance humanity?
- What does mankind need from me?
- Who have I been a blessing to lately?
- How can I reach those in need?

Answers?

Toni Osborne

Let your life make the difference in someone else's.

Whether our exchange with someone is positive or negative, it is significant and reflective of who we are at our core. Determine that what you yield will not contribute to anyone's stagnation, but will instead jettison foolishness and quicken purpose. Let your impartation linger in such a way that its captive will not be freed by your exit, and its manifestation will be eagerly multiplied.

Along our life's journey, the people whose paths we cross will be innumerable.

More will go unnoticed than not.

Many will be acknowledged.

Some will leave a lasting impression.

Few will make an impact.

Be the few.

Don't judge, discern; and in that, be diligent and deliberate.

Don't be so quick to condemn the state of affairs of other people. You don't know what their plight has been, what they've overcome, endured, or struggle with. You don't know what led them to their current status, and you don't know where you'd be if your journey thus far, had been the same.

In addition to that, don't fashion yourself more worthy than others, because you are where you are by the grace of God only, and subsequently, you are held to a higher calling. "To whom much is given much is required" (Luke 12:48) —remember that.

Here's the point I'm making:

It's not our place to enforce what others should or should not be doing, however, the responsibility of removing ourselves from environments that aren't conducive to our well-being, falls squarely on our shoulders. Therefore in exercising discernment, evaluate yourself, which in relation to your values and core beliefs, will help you determine what things would be unproductive inclusions in your life, with the potential to compromise your best interests.

Make these decisions on purpose, but have compassion for others in the expression of your choices. You don't have to berate people with your viewpoint to stand strong in your convictions, but you do need to definitely have some.

Influence is best not abandoned.

I would bet good money (oxymoron; isn't all money good? Okay, I know better. My good vs. evil is acting up again. Now where was I?)

I'd bet money that at least once in your life you've imagined a massive audience watching you do something you believed would cause them to idolize you forever; something that would leave them in awe of you. I've had several such thoughts. Once, I was tap dancing, another time playing the piano, then there's the time I was acting... doing my one-tear rendition of Demi Moore in Ghost. And oh yeah, there was that time I was doing a stand-up comedy routine (I really think I had a shot at this one— you're laughing! See, you're laughing!)

I know, I know, delusions of grandeur, but they're helping me get to the moral of the story:

You don't have to save yourself for the crowd!

Every day, you get the chance to leave someone in awe of you, as the potential to influence everyone you encounter, is always there. Each of us is a developmental instrument for one another, and odds are we'll leave each other with something. The question is what will that something be?

Don't let your influence just happen, but bestow it purposefully for the good of others because it is relevant, potent, and powerful! Don't take a backseat to this power. Know what you intend to leave and leave it! Like it or not, you model a role for all those in observance, and willing or not, your example *will* be set.

What will your example be?

What they see is what you get.

Of course, there's an exception to every rule and due to that, not everyone who witnesses poor behavioral patterns in their environment will adopt them. Nevertheless, we should make it a goal to model the behavior we'd like to see others exhibit, just in case.

We have the power to display what we'd like to see others become.

Create the standard.

Set the example by being the mother, father, son, daughter, friend, sister, brother, spouse, boss, citizen, *person*, and on and on, that you'd like to see others be. Be steadfast, as consistency is the key element here. It has to become a way of life for you if those in observance are to establish confidence in it, and follow suit.

Lastly, if you find you're not too crazy about the behavior you're seeing in others around you, take stock of yourself. You may discover it's your own reflection.

Commend generosity.

Not enough can be said about adopting a spirit of gratitude. Being grateful *for* and *in* all things helps us to become humble, and keeps us in the proper state of mind. This is especially true when it comes to thanking others, as being grateful for their efforts should inspire us to acknowledge and salute their contributions.

Encourage them with words and deeds of appreciation.

Motivate them with the truth of their impact.

Strengthen them with your affirmation.

Reassure them along their journey (as committing to *anything* is an act to be renewed daily).

You don't have to write their names across the sky, but somehow, let them know that what they've done is highly valued, and what they do makes a difference in the world. You never know how many more causes they'll be inspired to promote because you energized them, and here's food for thought:

It may not be a person's intention to gain recognition for the things they do, but it will surely give them a good feeling if it happens anyway.

Success is a collaborative effort.

If you're reading this you've lived long enough to be well aware of the importance of combining forces. All your life there has been someone, at some point, on hand to help you. From changing diapers to bandaging bruises, from establishing structure to cheering you on, much, if not all of what you've done in your life has been with the assistance of others. You had help!

I'm belaboring the point to make another. If help is required for the achievement of even the smallest tasks, why set out on any venture without your most valuable asset? Likewise, never get so caught up in your own talents that you fail to recognize the gift to *you* in the talents of others.

When you seek and at the very least accept the support of others, it helps to shoulder some of the burden. Do yourself a favor and not view it as an acquiescence of power, but instead, as an exploration of the wondrous creativity and refreshing new ideas that can come from such collaboration.

By the way, I know you're strong and powerful, resourceful, and very independent; you're no damsel in distress! Still, there are times when you must ask for the help you need, and not let your ego get in the way of you receiving it.

Toni Osborne

Social Journal

Social Journal

CHAPTER 3

Mental

Change is inevitable. To resist it prohibits
the positivity of its occurrence.

Resistance is understandable given the comfortability that exists in the routine, and monotony desirable, considering the reliability of the usual. Be that as it may, you cannot allow the security of the familiar to falsely lead you into believing that evolution is the enemy, and a new horizon is not to be appreciated.

Always remember: Your fighting against what *will* be will keep you from receiving the benefit of the transition.

What in your life is currently on a path toward change?

"Meant to be" happens. If it doesn't, it wasn't.

What if you had gotten what you'd hoped for?

Don't be disappointed for too long when something
doesn't go the way you want it to. Find your
resolve in knowing it's for your good, and that
in time that very truth will be revealed.

What did you want that you now see how you benefitted
from *not* getting?

Toni Osborne

Negative thought breeds negative talk.

Have things ever gotten so bad that you didn't bother to complain because you couldn't see the point? Did you get so busy trying to keep the sky from falling that you had no time to complain? Was your focus only on solving the problem?

Whether or not that's how you handled it, I implore you to adopt this philosophy in every challenging situation that arises, big or small.

Hear me out. I'm not discounting your hardship, but in order to resolve a problem you must pull yourself together and develop a plan. At the top of that list of steps should be:

A), **No complaining**. Verbalize the issue with someone who won't magnify it and is empathetic; letting you vent to release your angst but also objective, and won't participate in exacerbating the problem by entertaining your complaining. This leads me to B), assess how the situation could be worse and C), thank God it isn't.

When you do this you will begin to feel less entitled to perfect conditions, and grateful for conditions that aren't as bad as they could be. This mindset will renew your focus and move you to a place of solving the problem, as opposed to sulking over it through your complaints.

Synonymously, what you think has everything to do with what you say; that's why it's deathly important to have your thoughts in the right place, as every word you utter will follow suit. Remember this motto:

Your thoughts = your words = your reality, so whatever you say, make it positive!

Perfect time meets its demand.

Do you often hear people say how they can't wait for this or they can't wait for that? Do you witness how frustrated people become when they are made to wait? Hopefully, those people are recovering "I can't waiters" like myself, since the reality is we can and will wait when we have to. Having an "I can't wait" mentality sponsors anxiety and restlessness. It steals the present right out from under us because we're fixated on the future we're waiting for.

Due to our humanness, an "I can't wait" mentality is understandable, but I urge you to adopt an "I'm looking forward to it" disposition instead. This allows you to anticipate what you're hoping for in a calm, settled, and reassured state of mind. It helps you appreciate where you are, while letting your hope for what has *yet* to come, flourish. Besides, if you want what God has for you (which will always be better than your plan) you must be patient and allow for His perfect timing. And, since He's the author of time, who better to meet its demands?

Thing is, even if you're able to coerce a quicker outcome, you won't have the joy in it that you would've had if you'd waited. More than that, you may not be prepared to receive it and therefore not able to maintain it; haste really does make waste.

In the meantime, isn't there something you should be doing in preparation? And finally, when all is said and done the old adage rings true … anything worth having is worth waiting for.

> ***In order to reach our full potential, we must be
> willing to implement the changes necessary to get
> beyond those parts of ourselves that limit us.***

Take a true assessment of who you are and how you function in the world. After a review of all the areas of your life, you're likely to see the need for self-improvement. It is my hope that the list of things you love about yourself is the longest, but that does not negate the intrinsic existence of negative traits that we all have; that we *all* should be adamantly working to rid ourselves of.

Additionally, in grasping that the process of personal growth and development is lifelong, be patient with yourself in changing, but expectant nonetheless of lasting change. It's a magnificent journey for those who embrace it because they soon discover that the greater they become, all the more greatness shall they elicit.

The contemplation of a task is a defeatist act.

I distinctively remember a television commercial where a group of corporately dressed "think tankers" were standing on a sidewalk surrounding a trash can, discussing picking up a piece of trash and putting it in the can. They debated the matter until a guy in sneakers toting a backpack and wearing headphones walked by, picked up the piece of trash, and tossed it into the can without missing a beat, while the intellects continued to *discuss* the problem. Needless to say, the underlying message made quite an impact on me, and in the piercing words of a great Nike campaign, I realized what it meant to "just do it."

Moral of the story ...

Whether or not others fulfill their duties doesn't diminish your obligation to fulfill yours, so don't lose focus by comparing your actions to the actions of others. By the same token, don't be trapped by the limits of doing what you feel, because some projects will never inspire completion.

Orient yourself to becoming a taskmaster and as the tasks are laid before you, tackle them. Don't procrastinate or perform your tasks begrudgingly, instead with spirited acceptance, or better yet, manipulated delegation (smile), get things done!

How long have you been putting it off?
What is it, anyway?

Mental Journal

Mental Journal

.

CHAPTER 4

Emotional

It doesn't matter "why"—it only matters "that."

There is a reason for everything; including the reason you won't ever know the reason for everything—but I don't know that reason☺.

Some things just *are,* and in light of that, don't get bogged down with the details. What you currently know of a situation may be upsetting enough, so don't abuse yourself by seeking supplementary information that will further antagonize you, and ultimately not make any difference in the circumstance or its outcome. Honestly, when you know enough to make an informed decision, extra details serve only to set you up for an even more burdensome reality.

The gist of it is this, you need the information that will help you cultivate your bottom line, and you should consider any additional information a nuisance; understanding that everything you need to know will be revealed to you in perfect time and without manipulation. In this, you can place your resolve.

If you know what you *need* to know, what else do you need to know?

When it's over, let it be over.

Things come to an end. Not everything, but many things come to an end. Concerning relationships, it is extremely difficult to separate from those with whom our hearts have connected, but when conditions dictate that a disconnection would be for the betterment of all involved, the end may be necessary. As we mature emotionally, we learn to do what is necessary.

Understand that not everyone is meant to enter your life and remain in your life for all of your life, and that each person during the time they're with you, serves a purpose that was intended for you; their entrance and/or exit is no accident, nor has it happened per chance. Therefore, when the time comes for you to end a relationship, no matter its nature, do it. Yes it will be hard, but do it anyway. **Let go!**

You see, when you free someone you also set yourself free, so if they step away, you step aside. And, if somehow they turned out to be crazy enough to kiss *you* goodbye, find a happy dance and *do* it; you have no idea what you've been spared!

T. D. Jakes said it best: *"When people can walk away from you, let them walk."*

Aside from yourself, who do you need to set free?

When we allow our sensitivities to abate our objectivity, we are disserviced.

When people criticize you take it personally because it's personal; it's about you. It would be great if everyone would say the right words or do the right things to express an issue they have with us, but most times, that isn't how it goes. Actually, they often gravitate toward revealing their observation of us in a way that causes us to resist receiving it. I know, it's not very effective, but that's what they do.

Due to this, you most likely won't approve of the way a criticism is delivered, but despite that, I challenge you to rise above the negative feelings criticism may engender, and listen to the message. Although you may not like it, it can benefit you to be reproved because it can help to keep you informed, as we all at times lose sight of how we're functioning in the world. It's good to have people in our lives who can "check" us, if you will, as they reel us back in when we've stepped out there too far and will do it whether we like it or not.

On the other hand, just because a criticism is given doesn't make it valid, so in keeping your wits about you (as opposed to becoming flustered by your emotions), you'll make a truer assessment of your guilt or innocence. If you find you're guilty as charged, make restoration, and if you're not guilty, try to help your critic understand that.

As far as the way the criticism was presented to you goes—maybe you can show your critics how they should express criticism by the way you criticize them about expressing their criticism… just a thought.

If you could control anyone; I mean *anyone*, who would it be?

Tick, tick, tick, tick, time's up!

Who was the first person you thought of? Names, please!

If you answered like the majority of the people I posed this question to, not only were you not the first person you thought of, but *you* never even made the list! As funny as that is, it's a sad truth that reveals how we want to control everyone and everything *except* ourselves.

This battle for our control will always be twofold because the attacks on it will be internal (our feelings) and external (people, circumstances, etc.). When we abandon the resistance of negative forces trying to elicit negative reactions, we give away our power. When we expend our energies in worthless attempts to control things over which we have no domain, we exhaust our power.

Several factors contribute to this reality, but the main issue is that we don't want to suffer the unwanted results of not being able to control our environments and everything in them. And, while that's understandable, we should be more leery of an outcome manipulated by our emotional infancy and contrived in the recesses of our imagination; failing to disguise the very thing this insecure behavior reveals—lack of control of self.

FACT:

We cannot control or change other people. We can express our desire for them to make changes, but that change is and will always be up to them.

**Our biggest challenge, and greatest feat,
is the mastery of SELF-control.**

Suffering does not warrant its infliction.

Marty Daniels once said, "Hurt people hurt people." As poignant as that line is, and whether I am conscious of the motives of my actions or not, my being in pain doesn't justify my causing you pain even if you caused *my* pain.

Once I realize that subjecting myself to you is detrimental to me, I must relieve myself of you and begin a process of healing. Unlike popular belief, that process should not include threats, acts of violence, vengeance, retaliation, or the breaking of any laws legal or moral. Try your best to skip the verbal lashing as well, but at least in that, you'll keep your hands to yourself.

If karma has its way we get what we give, so don't fancy yourself as the judge or jury of those who have caused you to become scorned; that will be cared for and it will be just, now listen to me carefully…

You have to be bigger than the pain you feel and bigger still, than the situation that caused it.

James Lane Allen said it best, *"adversity does not build character, it reveals it"*.

Which of your characteristics has been revealed through adversity?

Having to have someone is not love; it's obsession.

When it defies logic and refuses to reveal itself,
When it has surpassed selflessness and
obscured the border of self-deprivation,
When it discards good reasoning and takes rest in fallacy,
When it returns empty, seeking sustenance
from the very place it has devoured,
When it chooses to say and not do—it's obsession.
When it defines selfishness as giving in to an
insatiable desire to put first the needs of others,
When it repels duplicity with wielded truth,
When it digs low to build high,
When its best attempt to hold on is to let go,
When it's done whether or not said—it's love.

Toni Osborne

Eliminate anything and everything that taps into your Reservoir of Pain.

Sometimes in our struggle to get over it, we simply get on with it, pushing all our hurts to a place deep inside ourselves. It is in that place where our past hurts are stored, present hurts fueled, and future hurts anticipated.

I call that place the ***Reservoir of Pain***. I admonish you to opt out of nightmarish situations by relieving your life of people, places, and things if it becomes necessary. Additionally, it's difficult to move past things that have hurt us, so as you try to, don't stand for anything that remotely resembles what you've left behind.

Do what's best for *you*; choose out!

What is tapping into your sensitivities?
What must you do to eradicate it?

If time hasn't healed the wound, try forgiveness.

If it were true that time heals all wounds, there wouldn't be so many bitter older people. The truth is, there is no simple remedy for heartache and it will hurt as long as it hurts. As a matter of fact, it's not the passage of time that heals our wounds, but rather what we choose to *do* in the time that passes that either promotes or prolongs our healing.

Pain is real, and whether we choose to suppress it or inflict it the affect will be detrimental, as either one of these choices would serve only to exacerbate the issue. Of course we must release it, but know that we have the power to make that release a positive experience for everyone involved, by choosing to forgive.

The key to healing is in our thinking, and will be accomplished only if we take an active role in its pursuit. We must formulate encouraging thought patterns to help us get beyond being begrudged, and flood our minds with positive affirmations to keep us from dredging up scenarios that cause us to relive pain-filled memories. Not to do this renders us emotionally paralyzed.

After you've prayed, seek the help of others personally and/or professionally. Begin the process of relinquishing the blame of yourself and everyone who has hurt you; of forgiving yourself, and everyone who has hurt you.

Sweetheart, you have to set your heart free. Only then will you be healed.

The longer the pity, the shorter the party.

How long are you going to feel sorry for yourself? There is one pass and here it is: if you've been clinically or medically diagnosed with any form of depression, or a mental, emotional, or psychological illness, I respectfully exclude you from this message. As for the rest of you, what say ye?

Your mindset determines much, and its perspective will facilitate a positive or negative spin on the difficulties you incur. It doesn't matter if your trials are self-generated or carefully orchestrated by the dwellers in the pit of hell, you cannot afford to give excessive time or energy to any affliction, as to do so will keep you distracted and dejected; consequently, leaving you irreparably marred.

You see, although it's acceptable to feel sadness in response to a devastating event, it should never be made okay to wallow in the depths of despair. You must fight against pacifying your feelings or sulkily indulging in your problem and honestly, finding a solution requires a lot less energy.

You have to deal with your stuff, and if you need help with that, seek it! *Decide* that you will live your life the way it was meant to be lived—joyously!

Godspeed.

Emotional Journal

Toni Osborne

Emotional Journal

CHAPTER 5

Physical

Stay gorgeous by any means necessary!
(Okay, be responsible.) Tsk!

I appreciate the latest advancements in modern medicine, and I believe in the "nip and tuck" as much as the next diva, but if you won't perform the preliminaries in the maintenance of your God-given beauty, should you really keep that appointment with the plastic surgeon?

I know some things are beyond our control, and for those things, good luck to you in beating *me* to the doctor's office, but for that over which we have charge, we must take charge. We must **NERSH**. Nourish. Exercise. Rest. Supplement. Hydrate. *NERSH!*

Monitor the following basics and you'll be headed in the right direction.

1. **N—Nourish.** Regulate your intake, and overall consumption of foods and beverages. Investigate what's good for *your* body, and select the nutritional regimen that's best for you.

43

2. **E—Exercise.** Develop a routine of regular exercise. This is critical for your general health and well-being, plus, it'll keep you looking and feeling good.

3. **R—Rest**. Every day, make time to unwind, relax, and just breathe. The body must be replenished; rejuvenated. It needs sleep, so get some!

4. **S—Supplement.** Consult with your physician about your current state of health. Supplement as needed, and as approved by your doctor.

5. **H—Hydrate**. Get your daily supply of water. Water is your friend.

These five steps will send you well on your way to *your* optimal health.

Are you ***NERSH***ing?

If we were all the same, we wouldn't be different.

You are exactly who God intended you to be. There
never has been, nor will there ever be, *anyone* just
like you. Your blend is unique and was specifically
formed with you in mind. You were created by the
One who created all things, and He is incapable of
making *mis*-takes because He does everything on
purpose; giving everything He has made, its purpose.
Treasure what makes you exceptional. Accentuate what
is particular about you. Embrace your glorious design,
for it was made without flaw—or compromise.
By the way, those who are convinced of their own
beauty, find no intimidation in the beauty of others.

Toni Osborne

Physical Journal

Physical Journal

CHAPTER 6

Financial

For the ultimate finish, make the most of the start.

Life is not fair.

Some have more than you; you have more than some. Armed with that information, let's move on.

We are not responsible for where we start in life, but we *are* to be held accountable for making the best use of, and building upon that with which we start. By utilizing the slightest opportunities, taking care not to be wasteful, and leaving nothing to chance, you will undoubtedly come to the understanding that *everything* is a resource.

Your time, hardships, victories, defeats, family, friends, health, talents, finances, skills, education, experiences, youth, maturity, career, chance encounters, and anything else you can think of, are your resources!

Right now you have to take all you have and can access, and roll it into one big ball. Now take that ball and begin to form it into the shape of a step. Is it nice and sturdy? Good. Stand on it. This new height has broadened your view, and you should be able to spot a few more resources.

Gather them, and begin to build your next step. Standing on it yet? How's the view? Broader, with more resources? Wonderful! Gather those. Build the next step. Check the view and gather *those* resources. Do you see where I'm going with this? Now, build the next step, and so it should go with you... for the rest of your life!

What resources can you gather **right now** to form your next step?

Learn how money works, and make yours work for you.

First and foremost, get educated about the financial system(s) in which you plan to participate. Take classes, read books, and use the advice from people who walk the walk. If you choose to establish credit, keep it in good standing. Develop a system for paying bills and always pay them on time. Do not spend out of your "void"; instead, seek the help you need for your problem. After seeking trustworthy advice, start a long-term financial planning portfolio as soon as you start earning an income; stick to it, and watch your money grow. Do not overspend; budget. Give, invest, and save *before* you spend. Start every year with a financial evaluation that involves projections, budgets, and goals, and DO NOT live without an emergency fund.

Unless you want to take on other people's debt, never cosign for a loan. If you must assist, buy whatever it is outright to avoid possibly putting yourself in financial jeopardy or ruin. Don't get sucked in by those puppy dog eyes; attaching your credit standing to someone else's financial obligation is *never* a good idea, and if they've neglected to establish good credit for themselves, destroying yours is immaterial. Don't squander your resources, and never lend more than you can afford to lose. Don't link your finances personally or professionally with people who mismanage money regardless of their relationship to you, and under no circumstances give control of your money to such an entity.

Don't partner with anyone unwilling to legally commit to your venture, knowing that any venture that doesn't start with a legal process will surely end with one. (This especially includes love interests; just saying.) And lastly, know this:

Whenever you choose to be financially discerning you'll face opposition from those who are not, but don't let that bother you. No one is entitled to have their way with your resources, or have you extend yourself beyond what you've determined is feasible. And, if they choose to get upset about that, let 'em…better them than you. Touché.

What do you REALLY want?

A. What do you really want?
1. That thing you're always dreaming of?
2. That thing you're extremely good at?
3. That thing you'd regret **NOT** doing?

B. What are you willing to do to make it a reality?
1. Do you need to be educated in this field?
2. Do you need experience in this field?
3. In what ways do you need to invest in your vision?
4. What tools/resources do you need to get started?

C. Have you implemented solution-based thinking?
1. What can you create to solve issues in your life and in the lives of others?
2. What can you invent? What can you *re*-invent?

STEPS:
1. Determine what you really want.
2. Gather your basic tools.
3. Research what will be required.
4. Utilize your current resources.
5. Write down a plan of action.
6. Get to work.

Apply this process to every area of your life. Once you write down a plan of action, (the small steps you'll take to get to your big finale), the picture in your mind's eye will get clearer. The written word will make your dream tangible, and give you a format to refer to that provides direction, and monitors productivity. This helps you begin to see and believe you can actually do it!

Now that that's settled, begin to implement the steps of your ***written*** plan.

A setback is what Plan B's are made of.

Question: Okay so, who needs a Plan B if Plan A works?
Answer: Uh—nobody.
Question: Who sets out anticipating Plan A's failure?
Answer: No one really … except maybe those who intend to counteract it.
Question: If Plan B is so good, why wasn't it Plan A?
Answer: Plan A was better. Duh.

Real talk—

Plan A will always be better, but Plan B will always serve as a stabilizer during the reconstruction of Plan A. Plan B is an alternative created for the interim and a necessary safety net, as creating options gives you some control over what happens in your life.

However, I don't advocate giving excessive thought to a secondary plan, because all your energies should be poured into your primary… but I do love the idea of having one just in case.

Have a Plan B.

F A M I L Y ... Frequently Abused (by) My Individual Lustful Yearnings.

Is that the function your family serves in *your* life?

We were not born with a right to burden our family but on the contrary, with a responsibility to contribute to the joint effort of upward mobilization. As capable adults, no one owes us anything nor is anyone, including family, obligated to pick up our slack. When I take ownership, which equates to me doing what it takes to care for myself in every aspect, I am making a great attempt at living a well-balanced life and in so doing, release those who I would turn to if I needed help, to pursue their paths without the hindrance of my irresponsibility. #beabletoaffordyourlife

The thought process is this:

When all family members participate in leading productive lives not only are no resources spent on unwarranted disaster recovery, but room is made for the establishment of strong individual foundations, which in turn can dramatically increase the family's collective efforts. With forces joined, the family is then positioned to capitalize on lucrative opportunities that could subsequently lead to their financial stability for generations to come.

As a family, our usage of each other's resources should propel us to victory over great obstacles, and elevate us to heights only dreamed of by our predecessors. Take care to actively participate in the building of your family's legacy even if, better yet especially if, that legacy must start with you.

It is the family who sets the foundation.

Earn interest; don't pay it.

Before you try to keep up with the Jones' ask yourself:

Are any of the people I'm trying to impress paying off any of the debt I'm incurring in my attempt to impress them?

Maybe you haven't given it much thought, but we teach people to accept us for who we *are* as opposed to what we have, when we demonstratively place the value on ourselves, and not our things. Remember this principle every time your feelings of inadequacy pressure you to make purchases that equate to liabilities instead of assets, and know that falling into someone's good graces should never require you to make poor financial decisions.

Things don't make the man; Man makes things.

Don't expect someone to do for you
what you won't do for yourself.

Is there really any need to elaborate on this right here? I cain't (yeah, I said cain't) stand me somebody who is always waiting for someone else to do something/anything for them that they themselves can do.

There will be plenty of things you cannot do, but make the effort. **Try!**

In your attempt to help yourself, others will be inspired to assist you in ways beyond your ability. Your tenacity in striving toward what you would like to accomplish will motivate them to contribute to the cause of you reaching your goals.

You know what you *can* do, so what things if any, do you need help with?

Be dependent on independence.

We fail ourselves at times, so that should make us cognizant of others' potential to likewise fail us. I don't recommend the expectance of failure, but I do suggest that the element of surprise be eliminated due to the shortcomings of human nature.

With that said, depend on people as much as you can without placing yourself in total jeopardy. Take charge, and be about the business of developing self-reliance. Set out to become independent.

In no way is this my attempt to negate the importance of combining forces, and at no time is this to conclude that we'll never need to depend on other people; we just can't let our dependence on *anything* supersede our obligation to establish and maintain self-sufficiency.

In other respects, you cannot live in this world alone and although it's bound to happen, partnering with people can be a risky pursuit, to which you must give careful consideration. Not so much about the union itself, but about how you will conduct yourself within the union as it relates to your independence. Whether the partnership is personal or professional, and regardless of the role you choose to take within it, always make the following a priority:

<u>Establish and maintain your credentials</u>- Licenses, certifications, contacts, on-going education, skills, and everything in between. Stay in the loop!

<u>Don't take a backseat</u>- Keep yourself abreast of what's going on in all aspects of your environment, and if you've elected someone else to lead, regularly ensure their trustworthiness.

<u>Contribute to making decisions</u>- Don't partner with anyone who *will* not or who reluctantly allows you access; knowing that anyone who would promote your ignorance or perpetuate nondisclosure, mocks the partnership.

While these are a few suggestions, there's really no sure-fire way to guard against things going awry. Nonetheless, make it a goal to find a healthy balance between your dependence on the involvement of others, and your reliance on your independence.

It's a dance … wear comfortable shoes.

Toni Osborne

Financial Journal

Financial Journal

CHAPTER 7

Intellectual

Knowledge is the gain of education through the experienced. Wisdom is that revelation, personified.

Knowledge empowers.
Wisdom endows.
Applied knowledge *is* wisdom.

Cheap is the new expensive.

What are you buying into?

1). Casual sex: diseases, heartbreak, abandonment, single parenthood, abortion, adoption, child custody and support issues?

2). Recreational drugs: lifelong addiction, desolation, and dysfunction?

3). Something for nothing: Scams, underhanded ways of getting ahead, and criminality?

4). The path of least resistance: shortcuts; easy way out?

5). Go with the flow: whatever happens, happens; let someone else take control?

I'll stop at these examples because I'm sure they make my point and here's my question:

When you count the potential costs of any decisions you will have to make, will you ask yourself if you can afford what you'll choose? Well, will you? Do you have reserves for the maintenance of your choices? Well, do you?

Chew on this:

Just because something doesn't require much from you initially doesn't mean it won't require more from you ultimately. It's your job to know if you can meet the requirement. Again, don't believe the hype! What may not have cost you anything at first, could end up costing you everything, at last.

Change is a catalyst for growth. Embracing change solidifies the opportunity.

Change is progress, and as we undergo transformation resultant of different stages and circumstances in life, we must accept change as essential for proper development, and most critical in reaching our anticipated maturation levels.

When we're open to evolving, we don't see the new reality as something that has interfered with the status quo, but rather as a chance to integrate the hope of what could be into the deep-rooted foundation of what has been.

Revel in change.

Are you hindering your metamorphosis?

We don't make mistakes; we make choices.

Learn from your mistakes or suffer the consequences.
Suffer the mistakes and learn from your consequences—that's better.

Mistakes happen to us, not by us. A mistake is an accident, something that just happened; it could not be controlled. A consequence is the unwanted result of something we *chose* to do. It's something we knew could happen but hoped would not; something we thought we'd get away with but discovered we could not.

Settle in, because we'll have to make countless choices in our lifetime and many of them will contain varying degrees of risk. We will make these risky decisions regardless of our prior assessment, and although our intentions may not be ill-willed, the outcome is still the outcome.

I know this is a harsh reality, but be enlightened by its simple truth; much of what we experience in life is due to what we choose. By the same token, how would we ever have what we truly want if we keep making decisions that will never lead to it? If you need a bottom line here it is; we could avoid so many of life's calamities if only we made better choices.

Nevertheless, take responsibility for your actions, knowing your input is often the reason for your outcome. **It was no mistake.** *It was a choice.*

Where there is no virtue, there is no integrity.
Where there is no nobility, there is no dignity.
Where there is no morality, there is no character.
Where there is no sincerity, there is no heart.
Where there is no righteousness, there is no honesty.
Where there is no reverence, there is no humility.
Where there is no loyalty, there is no trust.
Where there is no truth, there is no faith.
Where there is no authenticity, there is no credibility.
Where there is no honor, there is no respect.

We honor what we respect.

Time, like money, is an investment. Spend it wisely.

Would you lend money to someone you knew wouldn't pay it back? Then why give your time to something that would be all the more futile, considering you can never get *time* back?

There are only a few resources that once they're gone they're gone and time is one of them. You can't borrow, lend, buy, sell, trade, reserve, undo, make up, change, stop, or even steal time. Your best hope would be to jump time zones to salvage time, and even on a good day, that's a ridiculous notion.

Govern your time by this acknowledgement:

There will never be enough time in a day to fit in all the things you enjoy, nor will there ever be enough time in a day to fit in all the things you *have* to do. In light of that, place value on your time—first things first.

When we value our time, we accept that the management of it personally and professionally is vital to the success of all we undertake; prioritizing accordingly and making allotments as needed. When we value our time, we abandon squanderous activities, reject idleness, and shun fruitless endeavors like the wastelands that they are, opting to take full advantage of this hot commodity called time… getting the most from it by making the most of it.

What has your time?
Should it?

**Don't hold on for what could be if
what is will never allow it.**

You have to stop fantasizing about what you'd like
it to be and acknowledge what it actually is. Being
honest with yourself will be the first step of you moving
toward what your heart truly desires. In fact, it'll be
the only way you stand a chance of ever getting it.

Tell yourself the truth! *Go on…*

We mean what we do.

Actions speak louder than words says Aisling Limerick, and our behavior is indicative of what our priorities are. If a person's actions are not falling in line with their words, you must believe what they're *doing*, not saying.

Let no one confuse you with eloquent words, or take space in your actual plans with their whimsical dreams. Allow the fantasy they create to inspire you to never accept the proposed over the performed.

Intent is not tangible, and the truth is what gets done.

What are they saying?
What are they *doing*?

Toni Osborne

Age has not patented wisdom, and youth relinquishes not the expectation of knowledge.

No matter your years ...
There will always be someone trying to teach you something; if you're lucky.

No matter your years ...
Be willing to learn. You know a lot; just not everything.

No matter your years ...
Knowledge empowers. Wisdom endows.

No matter your years ...
Ignorance does not excuse accountability.

Victims don't choose.

You were born empowered, but to access your best life you must be awake to your power; aware of it. It is that awareness that causes you to be conscious when you make decisions, so as not to undermine your desired end. With that said, **choices are for those positioned to do so.** As victims, we are subject to the sufferings of happenstance; our control thwarted, and outcome otherwise determined.

Victims have no say over what happens to them, and the word *victim* is often inappropriately applied. In the same vein, when we have been overtaken and things are done to us forcibly, we have been victimized. Everything short of that we endure because we *choose* to.

Maybe you've never thought about it, but when you make a choice to endure, you eliminate victimization from the equation; knowing that at any time you are free to make a different choice. A choice conducive to a circumstance more favorable, and ultimately, up to you.

Are you a victim?

Decide.

Absolutely nothing can happen without a decision having been made. It's the first thing that gets done before *anything* gets done. It is critically important for you to understand that *"decide"* is an action word, and that *to decide* is to take action.

Deciding is a power position, through which procrastination can be stripped of its stronghold, leading us to our conclusion of what to do or which path to take. This enables us to gain focus and channel our energies; two vital components of any endeavor, and it eliminates the division that indecisiveness generates, which in turn, helps to establish a definite direction.

Do you realize how much you put at stake by simply failing to make decisions? **Do you know how much you risk when your forfeit your decision making rights?**

You stand to lose everything because you have stepped aside and empowered someone else to decide for you. Remember, not everyone struggles with making decisions, so when you don't make them for yourself you position someone else to make them for you.

So fix it! Take charge of what's going to go on in your life! Have an opinion about what happens *with* you and what happens *to* you! Do what it takes to stand in your position of power! Make decisions about what you want, and what you need to do to get there!

Decide!

Intellectual Journal

Toni Osborne

Intellectual Journal

CHAPTER 8

Relational

A barren source yields void.

"Nothin' from nothin' leaves nothin'; gotta have somethin' if you wanna be with me." What a jazzy tune by Billy Preston. I thought about making this page like one of those singing greeting cards ya know, but after witnessing myself in song, I figured I'd better keep writing—now back to the lesson. By the way, this concept even works out mathematically since 0+0=0, and the numbers do not lie!

Just because we want something from someone doesn't mean that person has it to give. Just because someone wants something from us doesn't mean *we* have it to give. It's time to do some homework. The math is done, so pull out your self-study workbook (your expectations) and your language arts folder (effective communication).

You are now equipped with the tools you need to evaluate what is feasible to reasonably expect from said source. Once it's been made clear by words, actions, or both that the source cannot render your expectations, it becomes at that moment unreasonable for you to harbor the same expectations from that source. If you continue to have the same expectations under these circumstances, know that you are now *solely* responsible for any disappointment you experience resultant of not having these expectations met. If it's not available, don't torture yourself by expecting it.

NOTE:

This is not to suggest that you change your expectations. This is to suggest that you change the *source* of your expectations. Keep it simple.

Friendship. Trumps. Kinship.

We don't get to choose our family, so we have to make the best of what we have. Having said that, being related to someone doesn't justify the mistreatment of you by them, nor does it obligate you to tolerate poor treatment, and in that vein, does not give *you* a pass to mistreat them. No one, not even family, has to put up with your crap.

To befriend someone is a choice and in so choosing, we decide to positively participate in that relationship with the understanding that to not, will likely result in the ending of it. Too often because we're family, we're convinced the relationships will never end, and may find ourselves not respecting them.

Thing is, if a relationship is valued we do what it takes to maintain it, as we often have a regard for our friendships that we may not have for our familial relationships. Unfortunately, somewhere along the line we make it okay to take our kinships for granted, thus the breakdown.

Let me be clear. Ideally, the people closest to us would be those with whom we share a bloodline, but realistically, they're just people too. Titles mean nothing when there's no relationship because bonds are formed where they can be.

At last, if you approach *all* your personal relationships from the "friendship" perspective, your kinships are sure to make the transition.

Are your kinships friendships?

Even in dispute, your heart must remain loving.

Tone and manner are crucial in effective communication; don't say things to tear people down, and don't do things to break people down. Exhibiting mutual respect will garner the empathy and understanding that is needed to adequately work through opposing positions. Moreover, being logical is not overrated, as emotions can often drive us to exaggeration of thought and in turn, fuel more emotion. **Do not react to your emotions!** Take a step back. Gather yourself. Think it through. Approach it.

In addition, having disagreements can be beneficial if we learn through them and grow from them. It is also very possible to have disputes without fighting or arguing, since those behaviors are not inherent, but environmental. *Release yourself from destructive patterns of resolving issues.*

Aggressive or passive, we are all to be held accountable for the state of our relationships and due to that, should be asking ourselves:

A). Do I perpetuate the problem?

B). Am I working to bring about resolution?

C). Do I need to develop and/or improve my conflict-resolution skills?

These questions are not rhetorical. Remember—the challenges of your relationships are coming, but even in dispute, your heart must remain loving.

The more you love yourself, the better your loving others will be. The more you are yourself, the truer their love for you can be.

Chris Rock said, "When you meet someone for the first time, you're not meeting them, you're meeting their representative." It's funny when he says it because my rendition *clearly* has no punch line, but never mind that, you get the point.

Be yourself.

Get to know you, learn to love you, and present that person to the world. It won't be easy and you'll be greatly tempted to be pretentious, but stand firm against that temptation, and be unyielding to its false sense of security.

Whether or not any of us will admit it, our grand cover-ups are usually the very thing that exposes us; talk about chasing our tails.

Do yourself a favor and spend your time being you. It'll be the best time you'll ever have.

Other people's dysfunction is just that.

How many times have you taken personally a problem someone was having, only to discover it had nothing to do with you? If you're like I used to be, it's more times than you'll care to admit. If you're like I used to be, you became so offended by the very accusation that you started defending yourself without processing whether you needed to.

This is what I've learned; not everyone chooses to process their pain in a nondestructive way and in fact, when our emotions are wayward, a tendency to project them onto others often exists. I cannot stress enough the importance of being self-aware, as it is the one tool to use in determining what the matter has to do with you.

When you use objectivity to assess an alleged offense, you can more thoroughly evaluate your role or lack thereof. If you determine that you are not a party to the issue, you must not internalize it; which in turn should stabilize your emotions. From this reasonable position, you should attempt to call to order the projections of the person offended with understanding and loving kindness; refusing to perpetuate any communication to the contrary, while trying to redirect them to the source of their concerns and a possible solution. Examining yourself first makes this outcome attainable and quite frankly, not everything is about you. Some things just are *not* about you!

If you can't find perfect in the mirror, stop looking.

Are you going through life expecting me to be what *you* aren't?

Do you really think it's not you, it's me?

How do you always know exactly what's wrong with me when you spend so much more time with you?

How 'bout this:

Since you're not guiltless and I'm not blameless, why don't we give that realization the miniscule attention it deserves by accepting each other's idiosyncrasies, and creating a diversion with thoughts of how splendid we both are? You like? Me too. ☺

I think it could work. If I stop finding fault with you and you stop finding fault with me, if I can have patience with you and love you through your humanness, and you can look beyond where I fall short in demonstration of your tolerance, we just may be okay. We just may be okay.

It'll stop when you stop it!

Once people show you they're going to be in constant violation of your boundaries, it would behoove you to remove them from within them. Acknowledge the signs as they appear, and let their culmination precede your exit.

As a matter of fact, know that you become responsible for your circumstances the moment you recognize that the abusive behavior of others will be prevalent, and that by remaining in the situation after being offended repeatedly, you become a party to further offense.

That's right. **With the exception of your being physically overpowered, nothing can happen to you that you do not allow.** Furthermore, if being overpowered is *not* an issue, and there are no other legitimate factors to consider, the trouble then is not with what's being done to you, but rather with what you're *allowing* to be done to you.

You have control.
When will you exercise it?

Girls see boys. Women, see men.

Young lady, may I talk to you to share this simple thought,

To maybe help relieve the pain of all the days you've sought,

A tender heart with loving words that soothe away your fears,

A gentle hand to wipe away your overflow of tears.

I know it's hard to open to these unfamiliar things,

To not know if the wind *will* blow and get beneath your wings,

But it's time to do the best thing for yourself you ever could,

To take the time to make sure that the man you pick is good.

The way he walks with you and talks to you and strokes your pretty face,

The way he looks at you to let you know he wants you in his space,

The way he listens with great patience as you stress about your day and as you speak

The way he takes his hands and melts the stress away. If he's gentle, kind, and interested in you, your plans, your dreams

And if he offers up himself to you—his heart and *every*thing.

But there's more to come 'cause that's not all a man will surely do;

He will protect, provide… love, respect, and always cover you.

He's strong and sure and knows that when you look into his eyes,

You expect with hope; you need and want what's real devoid of lies.

He knows his role; he heads this thing with you and yours in tow,

And if it makes you happy to be free, his love will let you go.

He's not afraid of you and doesn't have to rule by force of hand,

So you are free to be the woman because he knows that he's the man.

He'll dress you up and show you off; you're on his arm, a work of art.

He'll draw you near and keep you there, that sacred place within his heart.

You're special girl, but you've gotta know it—a man can only do so much.

You were created to be cherished; a unique blend that Heaven touched.

All by yourself, you're still amazing, full of gifts, and made from love,

As God begets in you the woman that *your* man is dreaming of.

The best is coming, so you prepare, as perfect time meets its demand.

You should be ready; vision clear—for only a woman can see a man.

Your relationships should be good. Period.

Bad relationships bring out the worst in us.

Good relationships bring out our very best.

The way we interact with and relate to other people has a direct effect on our mental and emotional states, which subsequently affect every other aspect of our lives.

Despite their nature, you must rid yourself of relationships that deplete you of stability in these areas, as you take care to protect your sanity and inner peace. Truthfully, sometimes personalities are just mildly conflicting, while other times people can be downright toxic, with seemingly one goal in mind—attending your funeral.

Make no mistake about it, when you connect with other people you get to see yourself—the good, the bad, and the ugly. What you see is who you *really* are. I know; sit with that for a minute. The beauty of this realization is now that you know, you can substitute your bad for more good so that it's no longer a point of contention in your relationships.

By the same token, what you see in others is who *they* really are and although you cannot change them, you don't have to let the regularity of volatile exchanges take place, choosing to exercise the control you have over how you relate to others, and how you allow others to relate to you.

Handle people the way you want to be handled!

So, instead of using sarcasm, bitterness, anger, and resentment to hide your hurts behind, or passive-aggressive silent treatments and secret punishments to inflict pain, take stock of what's really at stake, and be willing to acknowledge, address, and if possible, repair the issue.

Toni Osborne

Don't "conform to the norm" on this one; you can have relationships that are non-tumultuous and drama-free, if you so determine. And, if it's not positive, progressive, and uplifting, why would you want it anyway?

You are the prize. Keep your eyes on it.

What I have to say to you on this page alone is going to prove to be invaluable to you all the days of your life. **Your value is immeasurable!** If you've never heard that before, hear it now. Plant it deep down inside your heart, keep it there, and guard it with your life. Make this the opinion you have of yourself, and don't accept any opinion that does not agree with yours. *To have you is to have won!*

I acknowledge how important it can become to us to try to place ourselves within the good graces of those with whom we'd like to connect, but if to have that connection is going to cause you to lose yourself, it's in vain. I advocate the evolution of self-improvement and state there's absolutely nothing wrong with healthy compromise, but if they chose you thinking they'd change you, shame on them. If you change under that pretense, shame on you.

What I've learned is that the opinion others may have of me can be fleeting; it wavers and so, proves unreliable. What I've learned is that my opinion of myself must be unwavering; that I must hold fast to it under all circumstances, and be willing to go it alone, if only to preserve it. What I know is how easy it becomes to lose sight of *my* value when I place my focus on the value of others; placing the value of others, above my own.

I must admit that I am not a fan of having to say I'm sorry, and I flat out do not like to be wrong. And, while I find it liberating to tell you that truth about myself, I also know doing the right thing should not be predicated on my feelings, but should instead be derived from the factual assessment I make concerning an issue.

I know this is where it gets tricky, but it's imperative to make the facts the focal point of this assessment because without that as the objective, my emotions will never garner the humility that is needed to acknowledge my poor behavior and apologize for it.

Actually, if I allow my feelings to creep into the evaluation and create obscurity, I will find a way to justify my actions and nullify an apology. Don't be that person! Realize it's impossible to go through life without offending someone at some point, and know you're going to get more than enough chances to step out from behind your pride and humble yourself.

Needless to say, if it's not sincere, it's not an apology.

With that said, it's not my intention to lead you to believe that an apology will rectify the situation; it has great potential to but very well may not. And, as someone who once had an apology rejected, know that the honor is established in your giving it, not their accepting it. **You are not responsible for others' responses to your offense; you are responsible for *your* response to your offense.**

Let that marinate, and here's the takeaway:

Own up and bow down! Apologize.

Love is a gift, and as such cannot be earned, only given.

No need to clear the court. Your attempt to jump through that hoop will never cause you to gain the love you seek. Don't tell yourself these lies:

1. If I give my love now, I'll receive their love later.
2. If I give the best performance, I'll win their love.
3. My love for them will sustain all.
4. They'll love me back—eventually.

Listen, real love is interpersonal and will not be based on actions taken to acquire said affections, but rather the connection made from heart to heart. To boot, if you start by *gifting yourself with love*, it'll be that much easier to recognize when others haven't.

Aloneness is not being by yourself, but with yourself.

What better time to take care of yourself than in the still of aloneness?

The peace.

The quiet.

The chance to be in your own space, spread out; uninterrupted and uninhibited.

The room to heal, grow, and rest… from the world.

The liberty to be.

Don't be afraid of this time in your life; instead, turn it into a wonderful experience wherein you relish the splendor of self-renewal, the enlightenment of self-reflection, and the elevation of self-improvement.

Receive this blessing. Your aloneness frees you up to do something great for yourself and without guilt. Your aloneness forces you to retreat within and discover the treasures buried there. Your aloneness serves to teach you how togetherness *should* be.

What are some of the remarkable things that have come out of your periods of aloneness?

Be self-appraised.

Appraise- /aprayz/v.tr.1. Estimate the value or quality of. 2. Set a price on.

The world will try to pin you down and place a tag on you from the time you get here until the time you leave. Inevitably, you will be susceptible to the world's branding if your self-imposed labeling does not super-impose theirs. Your self-image must always weigh heavier with you than others' delusional estimations, so as not to erode what you must be certain is your worth. In this case, no matter what comes along and tries to convince you otherwise, you must be decidedly unmoved.

Hold yourself in high esteem, and at all costs, free yourself from anything in disagreement with your high standards. To that end, don't delve into behaviors that are beneath you, for that will obscure your mind's eye; displacing you from your pedestal, and leading you to believe you aren't worthy or capable of the best. **Don't do this to yourself.**

Be confident that your standards won't have to be lowered, because there are people with like minds equipped to meet them; wait it out. If nothing else jumps off this page for you, let this:

Stand strong and steadfast in the knowledge of your preordained value! Let it be determined by you always, and let it be determined by you alone! Well, I guess if you wanna believe what God says about you, that's okay too. ☺

Choose people who are enthusiastic about the opportunity to be in your life.

It is an opportunity, right? Just checking.

There's usually an overabundance of excitement as we embark upon relationships that often dissipates when we settle into their familiarity. The time that passes brings about a reassuring level of comfort and you want that, but without the complacency that can accompany it. Don't let being taken for granted become a staple, and don't champion the exhibition of lackluster efforts, with your presence. An "I don't care" attitude is to be addressed and evaluated; if possible improved and if not, removed.

Whether the relationship is new or old, it is imperative that the interest be mutual and that all parties are on assignment in its upkeep. You have a lot to offer; share it with people who will value you and appreciate receiving from you. And, if they don't see the chance to be in your life as just that; *a chance*, it doesn't change the fact that it *is* one!

If you're an opportunity, don't be an option. If you don't know the difference, neither will they.

You'll never outrun yourself.

You can "puff puff pass" until you're mistaken for a choo-choo train.

You can work until somebody calls you Bill Gates.

You can pop pills like a ferocious hailstorm.

You can gamble until you have no extremities with which to place a bet.

You can shop until the IRS comes knockin'.

You can sleep until the shedding of your fur.

You can eat until you epitomize gluttony.

You can drink yourself into a dried fruit.

You can have sex until the act is re-categorized.

You can smoke until you cough up a tar roof.

You can suck on that pipe until you headline the *Crackhead Chronicles* (JL).

You can steal until your fingers double as handcuff keys.

But after you do *all* that, you and your problem will still be together. These attempts at comfort and happiness will never provide it, but will instead serve only to perpetuate the very thing that led to your destructive behavior. *You have to choose to face what ails you.* **You can't fix one problem by smothering it in another.**

What's at the core of your destructive behavior?

Toni Osborne

Do what you say or don't say what you'll do.

I say this for everyone who has ever wanted to say to someone in particular, or everyone in general, who doesn't honor the words that ooze from their lips—**SHUT UP!** Don't you let your mouth commit you to another thing that you and I both know you aren't going to follow through on.

I don't know if you're overbooked, a people pleaser, an outright liar, a master manipulator, a busybody, or just someone who likes to hear themselves talk, but *whatever* it is has proven you *not* to be a person of your word… is what you want to say! And, furthermore! Just kidding; rant over. Oh, wait; you might be the person I'm talking about. Are you?

As problematic as this issue tends to be, one would think rectifying it would be associated with some lengthy program or intervention of sorts, right? Well, no it's not, and it doesn't need to be. **The only thing needed here is integrity.** All a person needs to do is what they say they *will* do after they've evaluated if they *can* do what they've said they *will* do before they say they'll do it. ***What?*** Exactly.

Just do what you say or don't say what you'll do!

Be a man of your word.
Be a woman of your word.
Word is bond!

**The only thing that beats having
good friends is being one.**

As you build your world around the essentials, do not neglect the necessity of friendship. In your good times and bad times; during your highs and your lows, friends will be there. When spouses, children, careers, family, money, youth, and everything else goes, friends will be there.

As a support system, they encourage, enlighten, and correct you as needed in hopes of helping you become your very best. As companions, fun abounds. Very rarely are people in the midst of having the time of their lives without the presence of friends. Whether enjoying new experiences or doing the usual, their attendance makes your memories unforgettable. As confidantes, the tried and true, you are safe to release your innermost thoughts and free to be your innermost self.

How better to return this gesture than in kind.

If they can't grow with you, they can't go with you.

This is one of the hardest things you'll ever have to do.

When you know what you want and decide to pursue it, those who are in your life and start out on that journey with you may not remain to see you reach your destination. It's like this, not everyone wants to live the way you want to live, and if they happen to, they may not possess the courage to face the obstacles that will be incurred. Their fears, jealousies, insecurities, and hang-ups are surely the culprits, but you can't let them clamp those hooks around your neck as well.

So how badly do you want what you want?

Before you answer that question, be aware that it may place you and them at an impasse, forcing you to choose between their needs and yours. Precisely; it is a costly but sometimes necessary choice to make.

When you set out to accomplish your goals and live out your dreams, your relationships may be tested as you would've never imagined they could be and because of that, may have to be re-evaluated.

As I write these words I do it with a prayer in my heart, because I know that what I'm suggesting won't be easy for you to do. *Do it anyway.* If your living your life on your terms, realizing your dreams, or simply living in peace is going to be impossible with them in tow—**unhitch!**

Don't wait OR settle. LIVE!

This quote could actually have found a home in a few other chapters, but I decided to make it "relational" because this struggle is real. *This* struggle has the capacity to make you or break you!

<u>*Here's the question:*</u>

Should you hold out for the person that fulfills your list of qualifications, or should you take what you can get among your current options?

I don't know about you, but during the time in my life when I asked myself this question, I couldn't answer it; nothing about either scenario appealed to me. I didn't have the patience to wait for the "qualified" person, and I didn't have the heart to break someone else's by not being fully engaged if I settled. I was in a pickle.

SIDEBAR

I didn't always know this, but so much of our identity can be tied to having a mate (or not) that we don't give proper recognition to our capabilities as individuals, or to the vast opportunities available to us in our periods of singledom. Like many of you, societal programming had me thinking the ultimate goal in life was to have a significant other—be in a relationship, get married, etcetera, etcetera, and etcetera. I've since grown to understand that after our relationship with God, our relationship with ourselves is the most important one we'll ever have. And, if I don't make *that* a good one, I'll be in no position to create a dynamic one with a potential mate, which raises another question: am *I* qualified?

Toni Osborne

I decided to *LIVE*. I've always known I had wonderful gifts to offer, as do all of us. But in my narrow-mindedness, I was limiting giving those gifts to a relationship, something that would never have the capacity to fully receive my offerings, because it wasn't designed for that. **Relationships were designed to *complement* us, not *complete* us.**

In my shortsightedness, I didn't understand that I had a duty to contribute my talents to the world and that even if I were in a relationship, that duty would still exist. I figured out that whether I'm single or coupled, I should be living passionately and generously; realizing that togetherness shouldn't solely be about having someone to snuggle up to, but should also be about shared purpose, worthy pursuits, real connection, and positive world impact. I learned that if I didn't have these things as a single person, I certainly couldn't bring them to the table for two.

This called for some serious self-development, and as a result, my thoughts became less about what I wanted to get from life, and more about what I wanted to give to life. My concerns became less about discovering a mate and more about discovering myself. My conclusion became to *live* my life, and in the pursuit of my purpose and passions, be open for opportunities in *every* area of it, with a resolve that knows that if I happen upon that potential life mate, I'll be ready. And, he'll be blessed!

Relational Journal

Toni Osborne

Relational Journal

CHAPTER 9

Passions

We cherish what we value.

Many a woman has longed for the day that she'd be massaged (I mean washed), oiled up (I mean waxed), listened to (meticulously buffed), and wined and dined (taken cruising) like a man does his most prized possession—his car. Limited-edition antique or old reliable, what a woman wouldn't give to be regarded in such a way.

Many a man would gladly trade places with a woman's coveted hairdo, for she'll lose many a night's rest to cater to it. No expense is too great to achieve it, and it will be placed on a pedestal (sometimes literally, lol), her love and adoration without falter, until death do them part.

Now, if we could just figure out how to cherish the people (like the things) we value…

> ***Every night, dream your biggest dream, and
> every day, awake another step toward it.***

Everything that has ever materialized started with a thought, a vision, or a dream. Spawned out of necessity, genius, or pure accident, it all came from hope actualized. We all have within us the abilities, talents, and unadulterated desire to bring something to fruition. We are all significant, and innately, want to express that to the world.

This thirst within us is undeniable, and although one dream may share in likeness to another, each one is very much its own—each one making room for the next. What's more, *we are abundantly creative!* We have talents of which we are aware, and with concentrated effort, other talents we will soon discover.

Search yourself day and night until your heart's desire is revealed and be relentless, for this bears no regret. Be persistent, for this bears great reward.

Have you discarded any ideas?
What were they?
Got any new ones?

A halfhearted effort will render identical results.

No matter what you pursue, your goal should always be to become your best at it. I understand that fully committing to something can be intimidating if not downright scary, and who at some point in their life hasn't been told, "Don't put all your eggs in one basket" or "Leave yourself an out." And, while that advice is practical and in some instances sanctioned, there will be times when the success of your pursuits will solely depend on you enlisting your blood, sweat, and tears—*your heart.*

Giving it your all will release the passion, creativity, and tenacity it may take to catapult you over any hurdles. Second, giving it your all will extinguish any thoughts you may have of what you *could have done* in the event you don't obtain your desired end.

Last but equally as important, giving it your all will change how you approach your endeavors; as it endorses a way of thinking that includes the expectancy of greatness, and in particular, yours.

If you're going to do it, give it everything you've got... **your all!**

Keep your flame lit by the fuel of your life's passion.

Your life's passion?

That thing you'd do if no one ever paid you. You'd get lost in it but wouldn't know it until somebody found you. Your thoughts of ultimate happiness always include it. It's your lifeline to serenity, and without it, there is no refuge. It awakens the kid in you with a level of excitement matched only by Christmas mornings past. Its void in your life could be filled only by itself, for *nothing* can replace it.

So tell me, what's your life's passion?

The meantime is prep time for show time.

Are you bored? No one's calling. There's no place to go. Nothing exciting is happening … blah, blah blah, blah blah. Is that your life?

Great! I've been waiting for you to get to this page so I could tell you this:

<u>GET YOURSELF SOME BUSINESS!</u>

Don't you spend another second sitting around wasting away with these trivial thoughts when you could be doing something the world *needs* you to do. You've been granted this time to produce, create, engineer, discover, invent, pioneer, explore, and a bunch of other words I could throw in here. We want what you've got, but no one can get it unless you give it! Use this time and figure out what "it" is. Take this downtime and cultivate your talents so when show time (opportunity) comes, you're more than prepared to step right into those positions designed just for you.

You will be given many opportunities throughout life, and prior *to* them, the time to get ready *for* them. Cherish the "meantime"; make it dear to your heart, lest a state of unpreparedness forces you to relinquish the impending good fortune.

Now get busy!

Ain't no way to get the high without riskin' the low.

Do you remember having any days where you cried out, "As soon as I _____, I'm gonna _____"? Think about it. What was it you were going to do to find fulfillment? How did you envision it? Are you doing now what you said then you'd be doing now? Has something left your fire only smoldering? Is it the daily routine of life, lack of resources, or something altogether different? *Are you simply afraid?*

Consider this:

In order to make real those things you dream about, those things you hope for, you have to take the chances they may require. Could it be that just the thought of what you'd like to do is overwhelming, and the steps you'll have to take in that direction seem insurmountable? If so, you have to fight to the death not to give in to that; that's fear trying to keep you immobilized.

Change your thoughts from how hard it *may* be to get things accomplished to how awesome it *will* be when you get things accomplished. Focus on the latter. Remain focused on the latter.

Accept that things are rarely perfect, and while every dream has the potential to go unrealized, it's all but guaranteed if you never try. So with these words in tow, take your best efforts and put them forward, and in the event you miss your mark, remember this:

If you reach for the stars and land in the clouds, you'll still be on top of the world.

You can't know true happiness until you know what makes you truly happy.

It's no one else's job to make us feel whole and complete. The responsibility of identifying what will do this for us is ours alone. If we're not willing to make time to explore who we are and what we're about, to learn what makes us tick or altogether stops our personal clocks, or to expose ourselves to the unfamiliar and open our minds to the seemingly impossible, how will we ever unearth what happiness is for us? If we don't know what pleases us, how can we help others know what pleases us?

Self-awareness is the key. In order to gain the insight necessary to determine what causes our elation, we must be self-aware. Once we've done this work, people should find us enjoying our lives because we incorporate things into it that we've discovered bring us fulfillment, and we eliminate things that have a tendency to deplete us of the very thing we're *all* in search of—happiness. This allows people (upon their entrance into our lives) to become another *resource* for our happiness and not *the source* of our happiness, as is often expected when we relinquish the responsibility of our contentment, to others.

What I'm saying is simple. If we don't take the time to earnestly figure out what makes us happy, we may inevitably waste time in situations that produce the polar opposite—unhappiness.

What makes *you* happy?

What do you really want?

No, it's not déjà vu! You read the same passage in the financial chapter, but I couldn't decide in which of the two to place this message because it's equally poignant, so billing it twice not only eliminated that dilemma, but allowed me to drive home this point that much more. So again:

What do you really want?
- That thing you're always dreaming of?
- That thing you're extremely good at?
- That thing you'd regret not doing?

What are you willing to do to make it a reality?
- Do I need to be educated in this field?
- Do I need experience in this field?
- In what ways do I need to invest in my vision?
- What tools do I need to get started?

Have you implemented solution-based thinking?
What can I create to solve issues in my life and in the lives of people around me?
- Determine what you really want.
- Gather your basic tools.
- Research what you'll need.
- Utilize your current resources.
- Write down a plan of action.
- Get to work.

Apply this process to every area of your life. Once you write down a plan of action, the small steps you'll take to get to your big finale, the picture in your mind's eye will get clearer. The written word will make your dream tangible, and give you a format to refer to that provides direction and monitors productivity. This helps you begin to see and believe you can actually do it!

Now, begin to implement the steps of your written plan!

> ***Develop interests that release your passion.
> Treat yourself well. Never compromise
> your core beliefs. Don't settle; choose.***

Need I say more? Okay…

Be involved with things that build your confidence,
improve your self-esteem, and make you a believer in you.

No one person has done every great thing. Your greatness, is awaited.

As we choose abandoned paths that destiny before us laid,
We should leave in its aftermath the remnants of a great crusade.
The first to dream, the first to plan, the first with vision you are not,
But love, you *are* the first to walk this earth endowed with what you've got.
You are equipped/Divinely purposed; the intention from the start,
Was to bring to light God's goodness while through you He touches hearts.
Don't get distracted by the struggle; forgo accolades and praise,
Just keep your thoughts affixed on those who set the bars you aim to raise.
You should be humbled but excited, if afraid, resolved to do,
All the duties of this task that its success compels you to.
Do not give up! Don't run away! Don't lay it down, even to breathe;
This is your life and it gives life; this is your dream, so dare to dream!

Toni Osborne

Passions Journal

Passions Journal

CONCLUSION

With my last breath this is what I'd say to you …

Absolute truth exists and is revealed in God's Word, through the Bible. To know these truths; to be convinced beyond a shadow of a doubt that you have received THE TRUTH; God's truth, is to be empowered in and through *everything* all the days of your life.

Be it unto you according to His Word
Amen.

LESSONS: THE QUOTES

Spiritual Quotes

Seek God. Find Him.

Falling into alignment with God's plan for others does not circumvent your blessings, it enables them.

A gift is not for the one granted the ability to give it.

Place your confidence in the Divinity through which it was afforded.

Out of the trial comes your magnificence.

In the moments with which you are blessed, be present.

Social Quotes

Action is not just for heroes.
Be inspired by others' desire to emulate you.
Responsibility constitutes freedom.
Ignorance does not excuse accountability.
Contribute your abilities in support of a cause outside yourself.
Let your life make the difference in someone else's.
Don't judge, discern; and in that, be diligent and deliberate.
Influence is best not abandoned.
What they see is what you get.
Commend generosity.
Success is a collaborative effort.

Toni Osborne

Mental Quotes

*Change is inevitable. To resist it prohibits the positivity of its
occurrence.*

"Meant to be" happens. If it doesn't, it wasn't.

Negative thought breeds negative talk.

Perfect time meets its demand.

*In order to reach our full potential, we must be willing to
implement the changes necessary to get beyond those parts
of ourselves that limit us.*

The contemplation of a task is a defeatist act.

Emotional Quotes

It doesn't matter "why"—it only matters "that."

When it's over, let it be over.

When we allow our sensitivities to abate our objectivity, we are disserviced.

Our biggest challenge, and greatest feat, is the mastery of <u>SELF</u>-control.

Suffering does not warrant its infliction.

Having to have someone is not love; it's obsession.

Eliminate anything and everything that taps into your Reservoir of Pain.

You have to be bigger than the pain you feel and bigger still, than the situation that caused it.

If time hasn't healed the wound, try forgiveness.

The longer the pity, the shorter the party.

Physical Quotes

Stay gorgeous by any means necessary! (Okay, be responsible.) Tsk!

If we were all the same, we wouldn't be different.

NERSH. Nourish. Exercise. Rest. Supplement. Hydrate. NERSH!

Financial Quotes

For the ultimate finish, make the most of the start.

Learn how money works, and make yours work for you.

A setback is what Plan B's are made of.

Earn interest; don't pay it.

Don't expect someone to do for you what you won't do for yourself.

Be dependent on independence.

*F.A.M.I.L.Y -- **F**requently **A**bused (by) **M**y **I**ndividual **L**ustful **Y**earnings.*

#beabletoaffordyourlife.

What do you REALLY want?

Intellectual Quotes

Decide!

Advice is good upon implementation.

Knowledge is the gain of education through the experienced. Wisdom is that revelation, personified.

Cheap is the new expensive.

Change is a catalyst for growth. Embracing change solidifies the opportunity.

We don't make mistakes; we make choices.

We honor what we respect.

Time, like money, is an investment. Spend it wisely.

Don't hold on for what could be if what is will never allow it.

We mean what we do.

Intent is not tangible; the truth is what gets done.

Age has not patented wisdom, and youth relinquishes not the expectation of knowledge.

Victims don't choose.

The truest indicator of one's capacity for learning is their acceptance of the lifelong process.

Relational Quotes

A barren source yields void.

Friendship. Trumps. Kinship.

Even in dispute, your heart must remain loving.

The more you love yourself, the better your loving others will be. The more you are yourself, the truer their love for you can be.

Other people's dysfunction is just that.

Own up and bow down! Apologize.

If you can't find perfect in the mirror, stop looking.

It'll stop when you stop it!

Girls see boys. Women, see men.

Your relationships should be good. Period.

You are the prize. Keep your eyes on it.

Love is a gift, and as such cannot be earned, only given.

Aloneness is not being by yourself, but with yourself.

Be self-appraised.

Choose people who are enthusiastic about the opportunity to be in your life.

You'll never outrun yourself.

Do what you say or don't say what you'll do.

The only thing that beats having good friends is being one.

If they can't grow with you, they can't go with you.

If you're an opportunity don't be an option. If you don't know the difference, neither will they.

Don't wait or settle. Live!

Passions Quotes

We cherish what we value.

Every night, dream your biggest dream, and every day, awake another step toward it.

A halfhearted effort will render identical results.

If you reach for the stars and land in the clouds, you'll still be on top of the world.

Keep your flame lit by the fuel of your life's passion.

The meantime is prep time for showtime.

Ain't no way to get the high without riskin' the low.

You can't know true happiness until you know what makes you truly happy.

What do you really want?

Develop interests that release your passion. Treat yourself well. Never compromise your core beliefs. Don't settle; choose.

No one person has done every great thing. Your greatness, is awaited.